Apple

Mela

Orange

Arancia

Strawberry

Fragola

Fig

Figura

Plum

Prugna

Pomegranate

Melograno

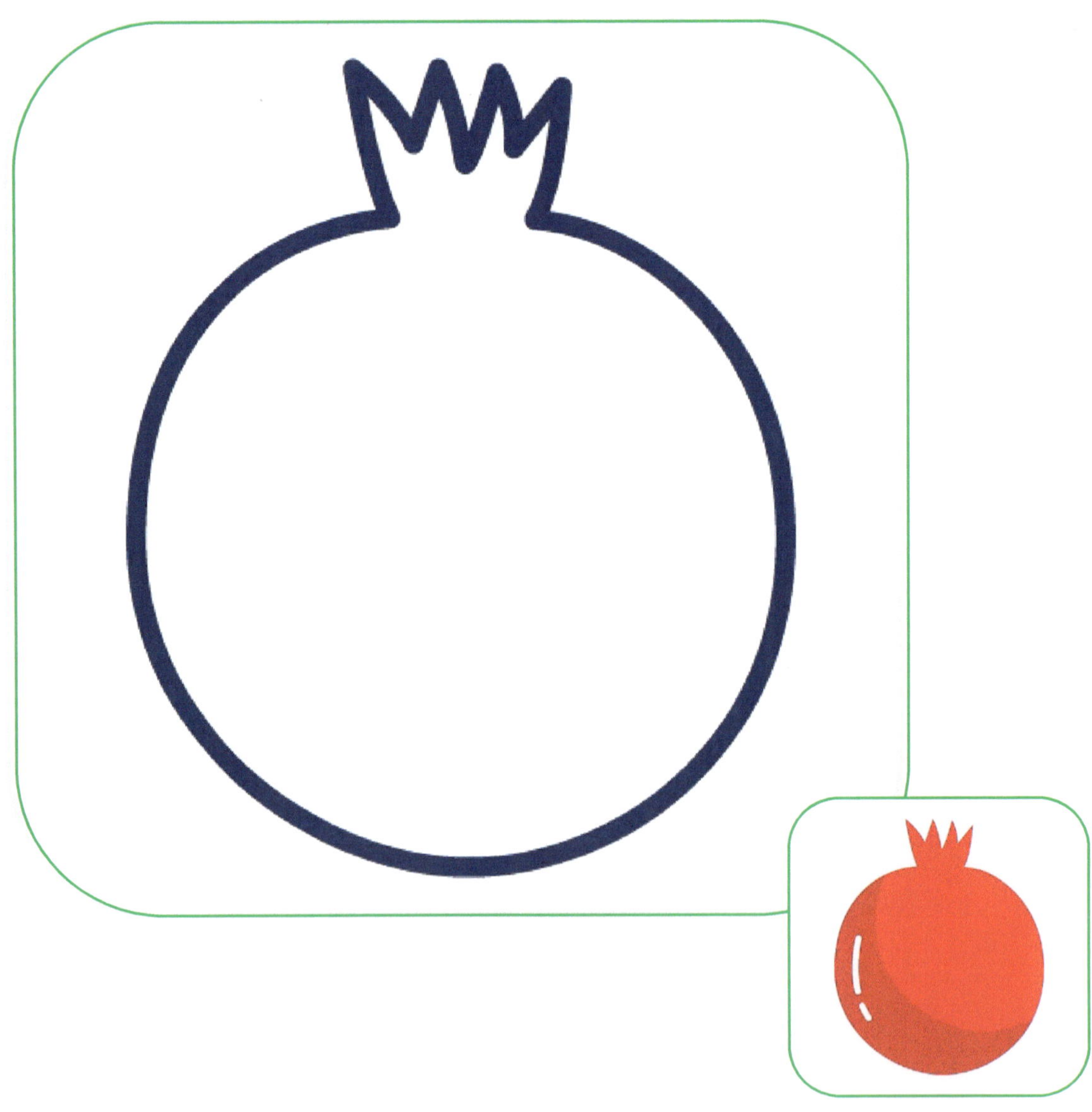

Clementine

Clementina

Starfruit

Starfruit

Date

Data

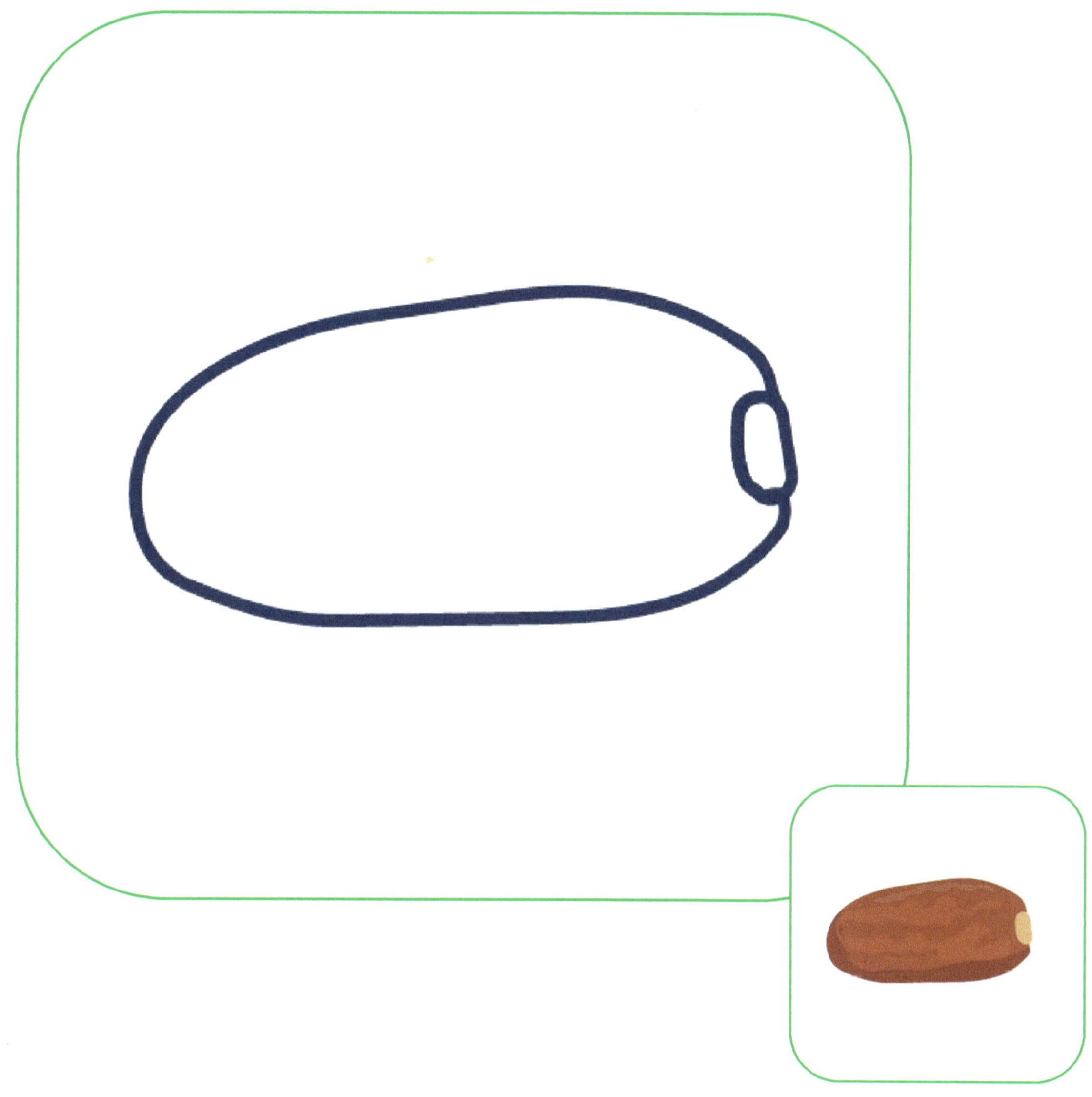

Kiwi

Kiwi

Japanese Plum

Prugna Giapponese

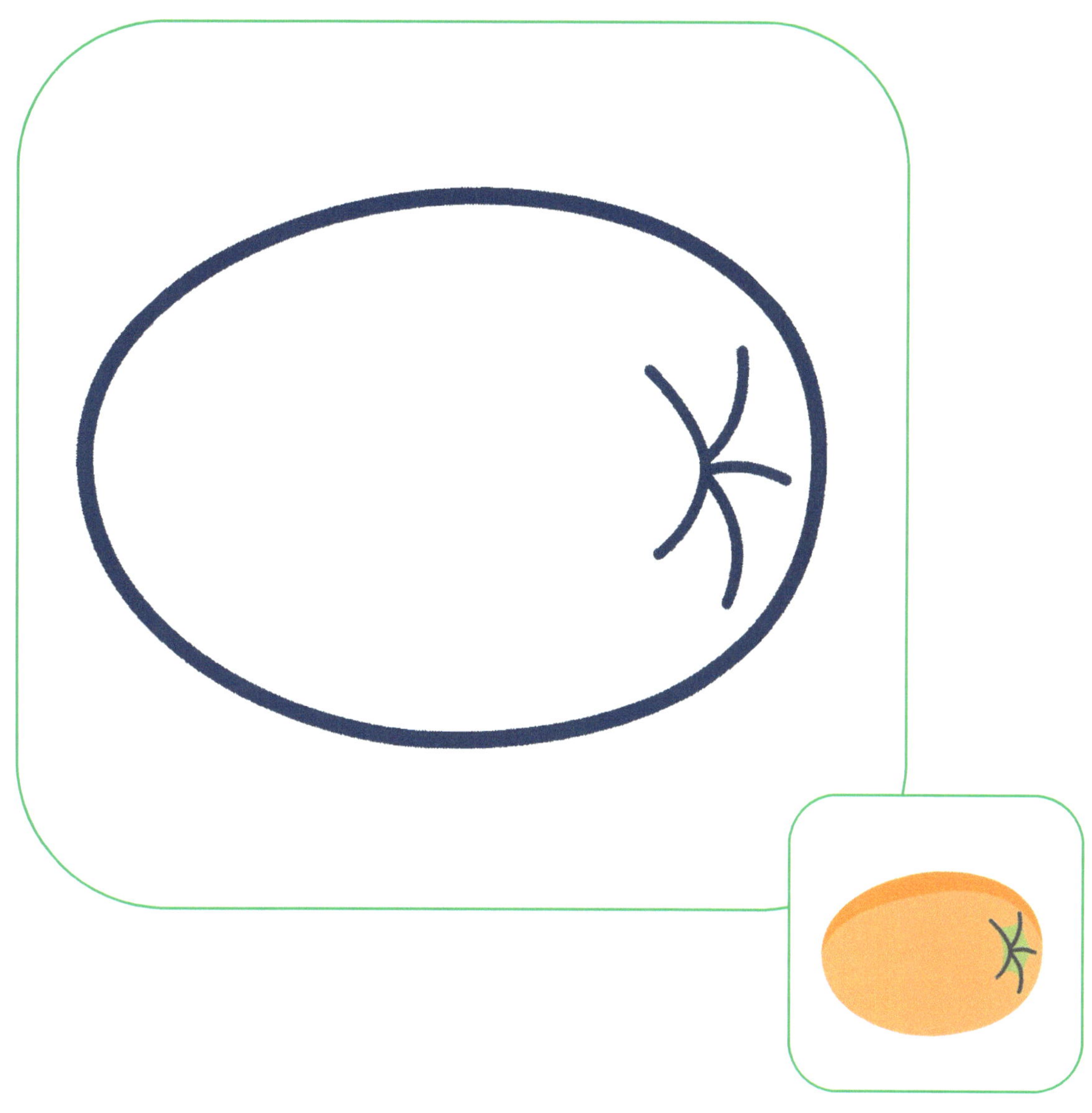

Papaya

Papaia

Passion fruit

frutto della passione

Pitaya

Pitaya

Raspberry

Lampone

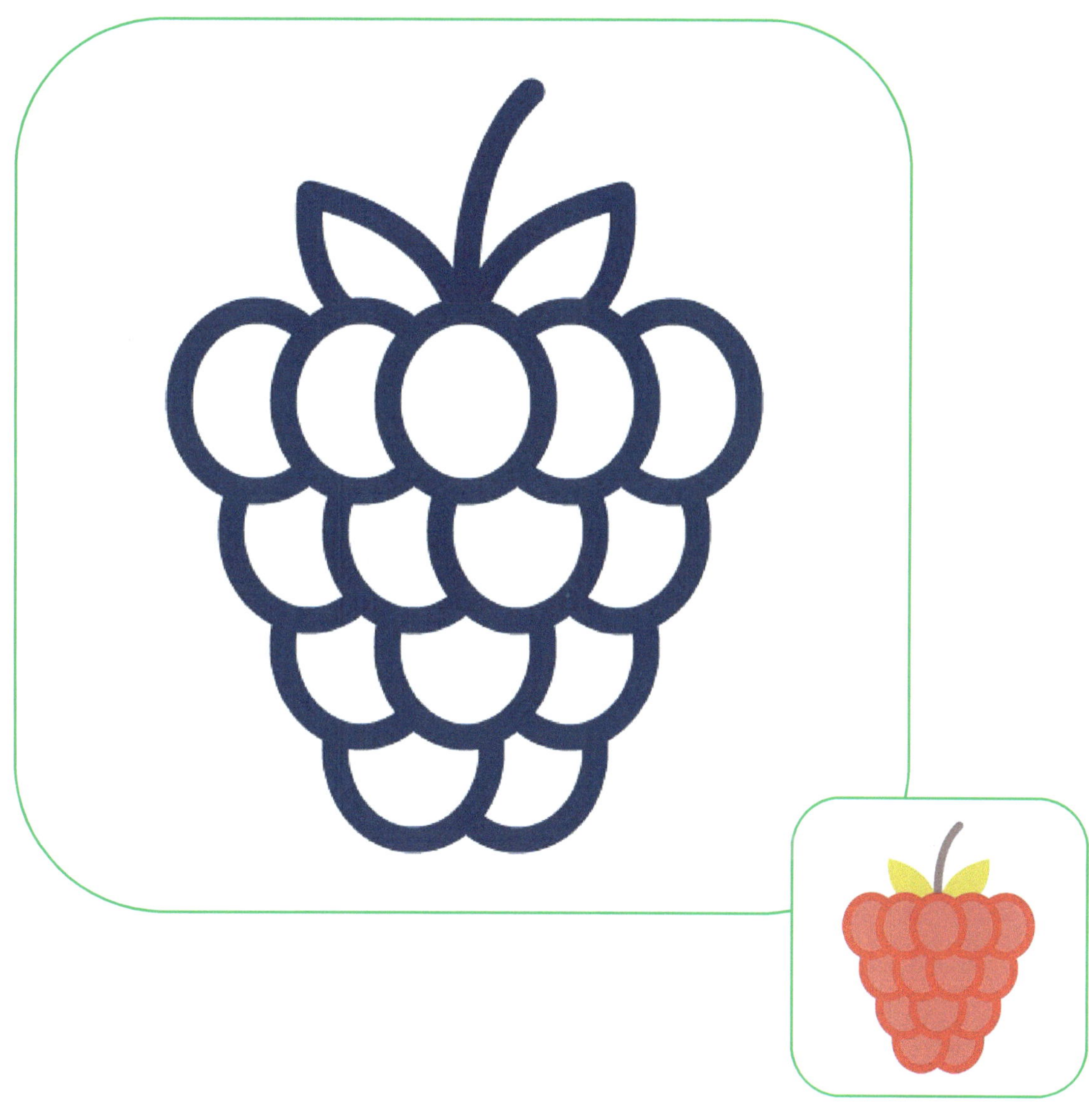

Pomelo

Pomelo

Grape

Uva

Prickly pear

Fico D'india

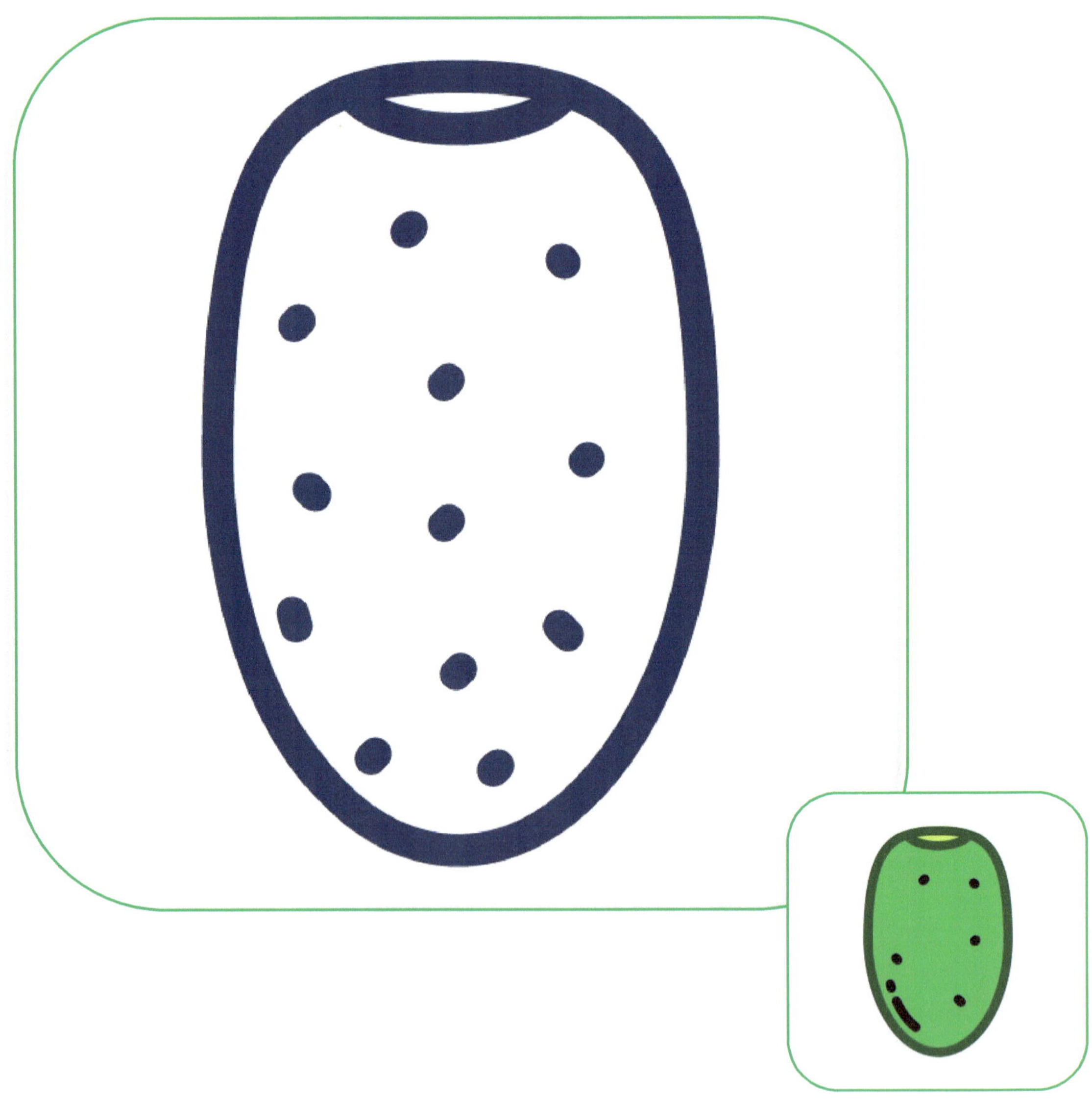

Apricot

Albicocca

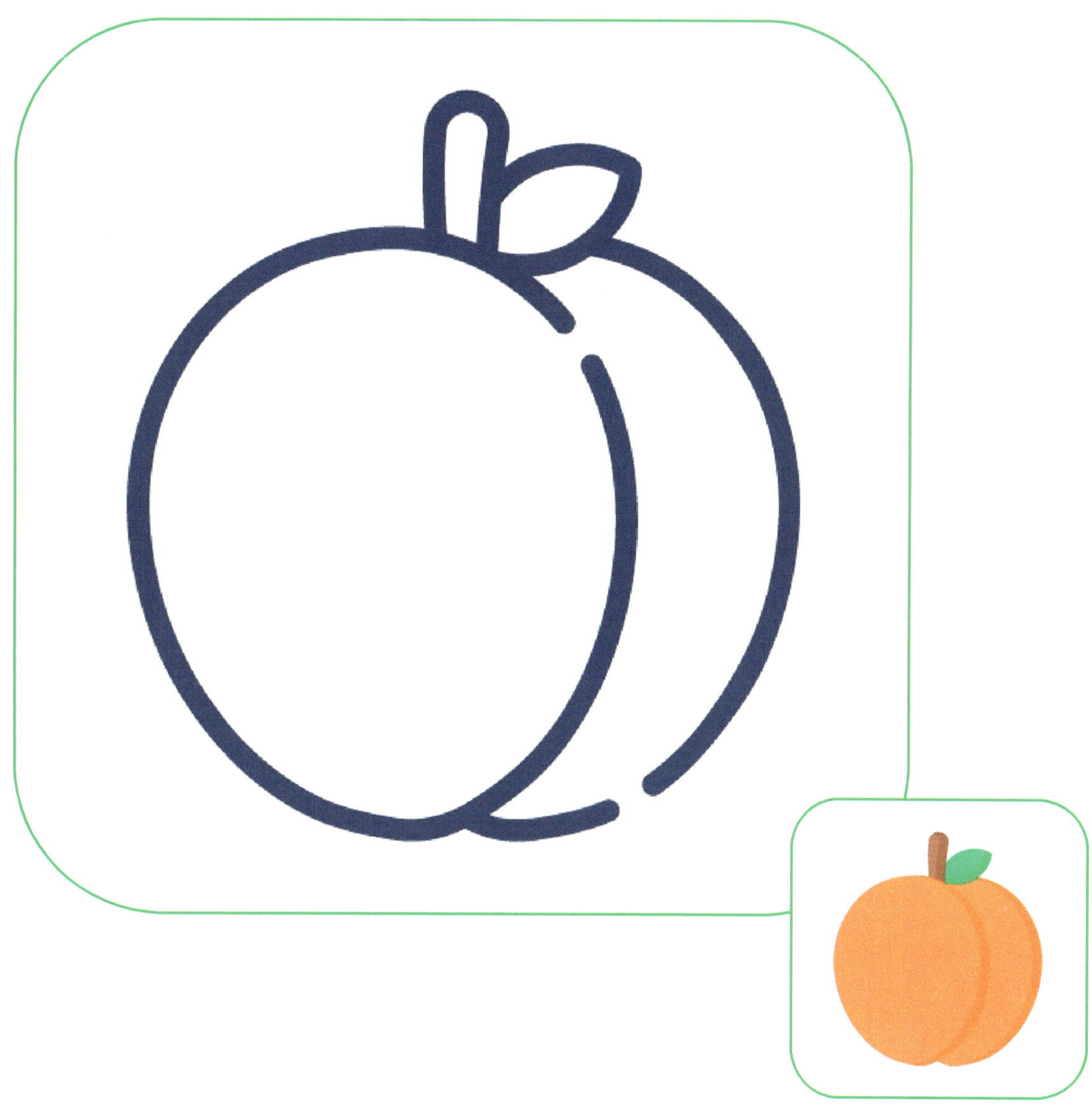

Mangosteen

Mangostano

Mango

Mango

Melon

Melone

Lychee

Litchi

Lemon

Limone

Lime

Lime

Cranberry

Mirtillo Rosso

Quince

Mela Cotogna

Olive

Oliva

Redcurrant

Ribes Rosso

Cherry

Ciliegia

Guava

Guaiava

Banana

Banana

Grapefruit

Pompelmo

Peach

Peach

Japanese Persimmon

Persimmon Giapponese

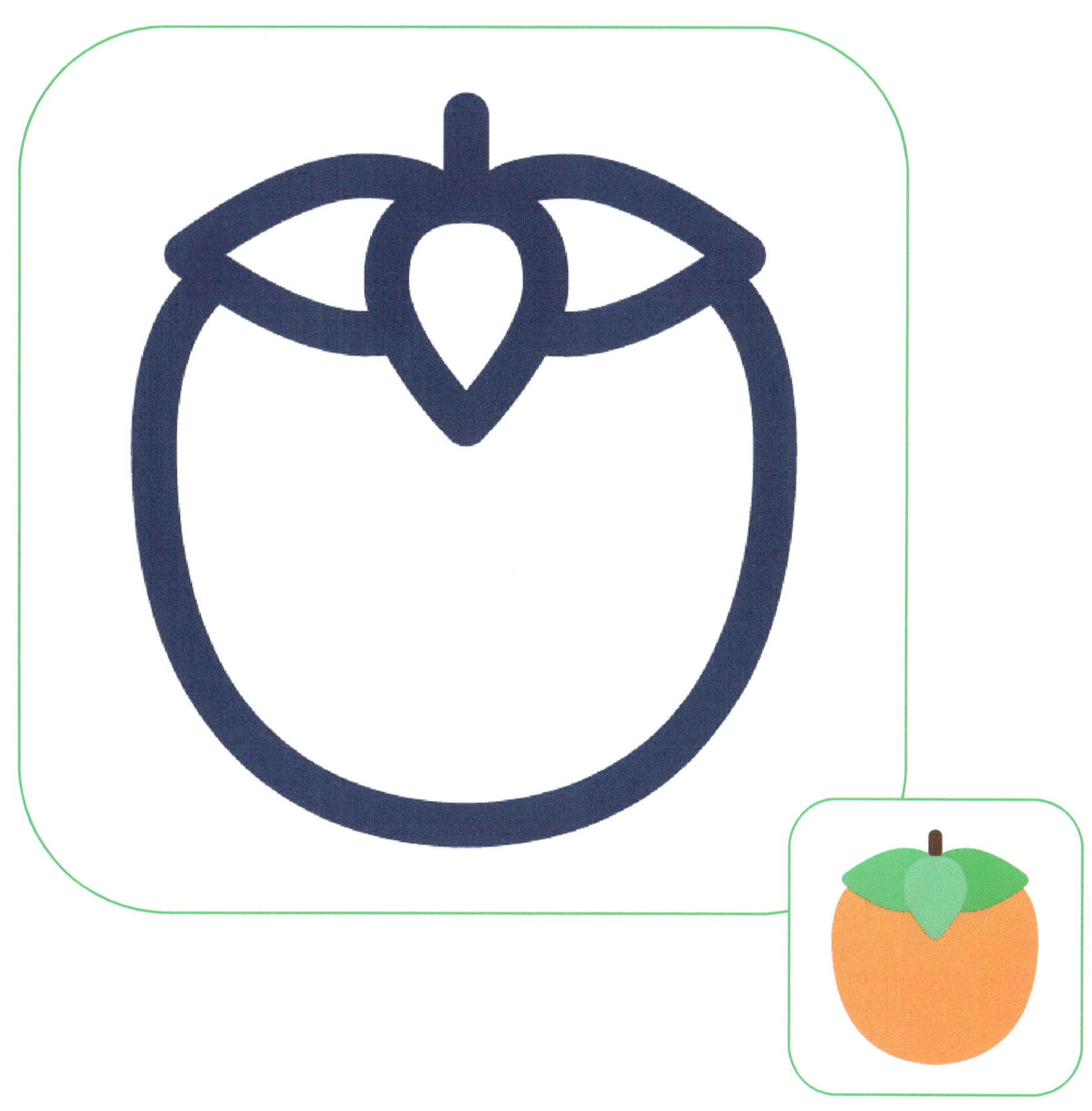

Pineapple

Ananas

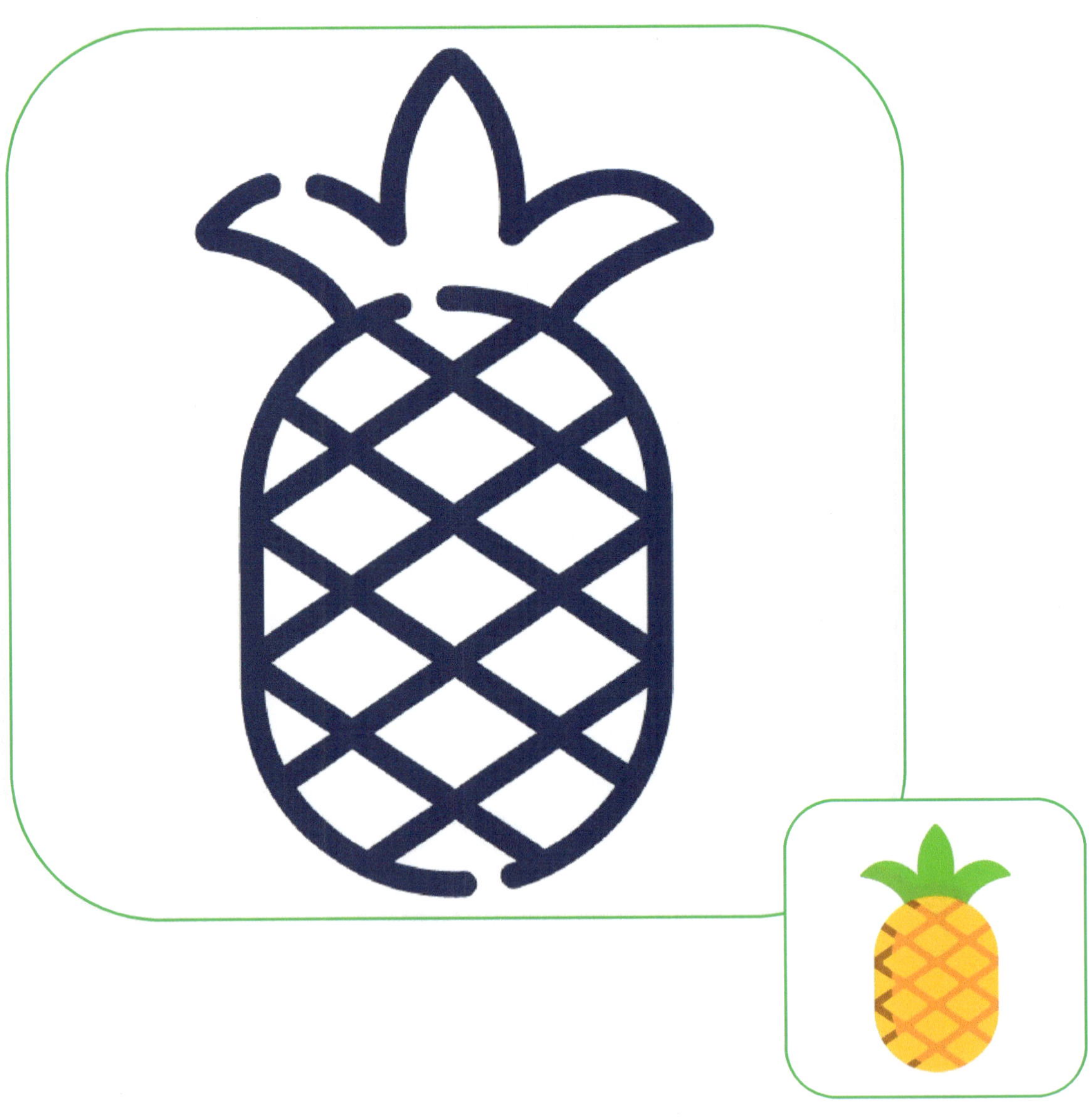

Soursop

Soursop

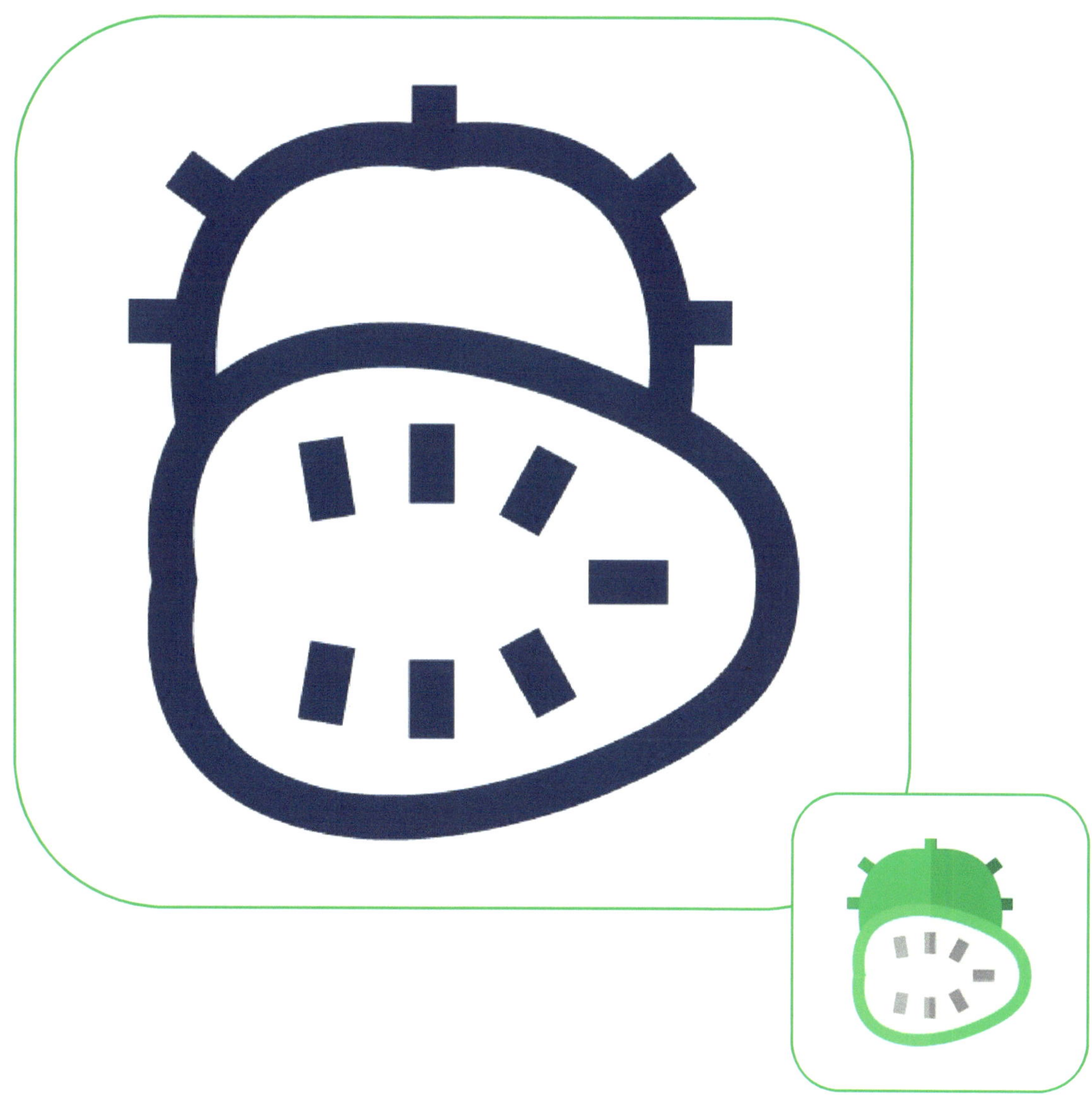

Blueberry

Mirtillo

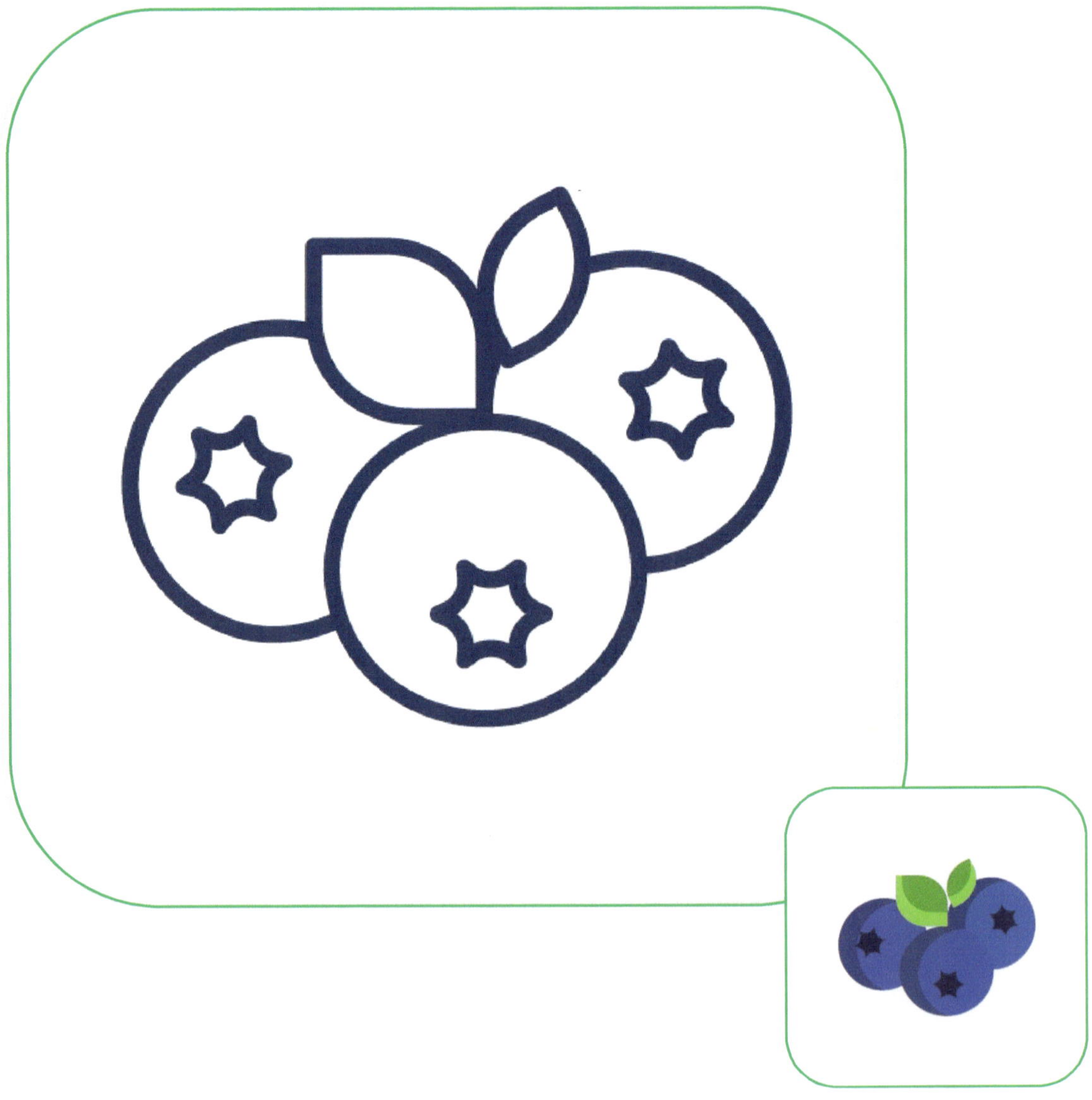

Pear

Pera

Watermelon

Anguria